MW01487396

5/26/17

Dear Sis. Manning,

Thank you for your
Love & Support!

— R.J. Chandler

The Little Book of Prayers

Invocations, Petitions & Benedictions

R.J. CHANDLER SR.

WESTBOW·
PRESS
A DIVISION OF THOMAS NELSON
& ZONDERVAN

Copyright © 2015 Reginald Jermayne Chandler Sr.

All rights reserved. No part of this book may be used or reproduced by any means, graphic, electronic, or mechanical, including photocopying, recording, taping or by any information storage retrieval system without the written permission of the publisher except in the case of brief quotations embodied in critical articles and reviews.

This book is a work of non-fiction. Unless otherwise noted, the author and the publisher make no explicit guarantees as to the accuracy of the information contained in this book and in some cases, names of people and places have been altered to protect their privacy.

Scripture taken from the Holy Bible, NEW INTERNATIONAL VERSION®. Copyright © 1973, 1978, 1984 by Biblica, Inc. All rights reserved worldwide. Used by permission. NEW INTERNATIONAL VERSION® and NIV® are registered trademarks of Biblica, Inc. Use of either trademark for the offering of goods or services requires the prior written consent of Biblica US, Inc. Scripture taken from the New King James Version. Copyright © 1979, 1980, 1982 by Thomas Nelson, Inc. Used by permission. All rights reserved.

WestBow Press books may be ordered through booksellers or by contacting:

WestBow Press
A Division of Thomas Nelson & Zondervan
1663 Liberty Drive
Bloomington, IN 47403
www.westbowpress.com
1 (866) 928-1240

Because of the dynamic nature of the Internet, any web addresses or links contained in this book may have changed since publication and may no longer be valid. The views expressed in this work are solely those of the author and do not necessarily reflect the views of the publisher, and the publisher hereby disclaims any responsibility for them.

Any people depicted in stock imagery provided by Thinkstock are models, and such images are being used for illustrative purposes only. Certain stock imagery © Thinkstock.

ISBN: 978-1-4908-7821-8 (sc)
ISBN: 978-1-4908-7823-2 (hc)
ISBN: 978-1-4908-7822-5 (e)

Library of Congress Control Number: 2015906620

Print information available on the last page.

WestBow Press rev. date: 04/30/2015

CONTENTS

In loving memory of
my grandfather Leroy Frasier

FOREWORD

I am very happy to give support to this work, *The Little Book of Prayer: Invocations, Petitions, Benedictions*, by the Rev. Dr. R.J. Chandler Sr. He is one of the up and coming young pastors in the African Methodist Episcopal Zion Church. His commitment to the mission of the church is unquestioned. Having taken a mission that almost died and resurrecting it to one of the leading churches on the Philadelphia Eastern Shore District is an outstanding achievement. I am sure that his success can be traced to his fervent prayer life.

Dr. Chandler is on the cutting-edge of what spirituality is all about. Prayer is indeed the key that unlocks the treasure-house of God. One hymn writer says that "Prayer is the soul's sincere desire, unuttered or expressed; the motion of a hidden fire that trembles in the breast." Prayer changes situations, circumstances, and people. If we pray right, nothing is impossible to us.

It is a pleasure for me to write this foreword, as the way of prayer is indeed a process. The disciples did not ask Jesus to teach them how to preach or how to administer the church. Their simple request was, "Lord, Teach us how to pray." In other words we must be taught to pray. For praying really does not come naturally, it is the by-product of the changes and challenges of life with a view that there is help available in the midst of our struggles.

As I commend this book to our church, my hope is that it will spark interest in deepening the prayer life of our membership. We are engaged in a very relentless spiritual warfare that knows no truce. Our foes are unseen and intangible, but they are powerful. As we study and emulate the prayers in this book, I am reminded that our weaponry is found in the prayer life of the people called Christian. Remember also that it is very true that more things are wrought by prayer than anything this world has ever known. In other words, prayer works. There are many witnesses in the Bible, as well as in our personal lives, who will concur that because of prayer they refused to quit and now are successful in their spiritual walk.

The Right Reverend Richard Keith Thompson
Presiding Prelate
Mid-Atlantic II Episcopal District
The African Methodist Episcopal Zion Church

ENCOURAGEMENTS

I am very impressed with this very practical book on the importance and power of Prayer. It was most moving as it took me through the meaning and purpose of each area of prayer. I was especially impressed with the section that dealt with the importance of the Worship Leader and how important it is that the person should be totally committed to prayer. I actually read the manuscript in one sitting. I do hope that this book will find its way into every church in Zion and beyond, and yes even in our households.

The Right Reverend Michael Angelo Frencher

Presiding Prelate

Eastern West Africa Episcopal District

President of the Board of Bishops (August 2014 – February 2015)

The practice of our Faith through worship, fellowship, prayer, intercession and others is rooted in the scriptures, history and tradition which were bequeathed to us by the Apostles and The Apostolic Fathers. In writing *"The Little Book of Prayers"*, the Reverend Dr. Reginald J. Chandler Sr. drew from such heritage, mindful of St Paul's exhortation "that supplications, intercessions, prayers and giving of thanks be made for all men; for kings and for all that are in authority..."

And in so doing, he came out with a rich and valuable contribution to the extant body of works on Invocations, Intercessions and Benedictions. I read the book with much delight and satisfaction. And I am thankful to God who gave the inspiration. With enthusiasm, therefore, I endorse both *"The Little Book of Prayers"* and the spirit behind it. But I commend the book to the young in Faith among us, especially student pastors as well as to the Theological Centers in Zion Methodism. In deed to our entire connection and to all else outside our connection everywhere who are engaged in ecclesiastical practice and service, as another excellent source of aid for ministry.

The Right Reverend Samuel Chuka Ekemam, Sr. (Rtd)
Prelate Emeritus, Eastern West Africa Episcopal District
The African Methodist Episcopal Zion Church
P. O. Box 1149, Owerri, Imo State, Nigeria

God answers prayer in the morning, noon and evening, so keep your heart in tune. Reggie, your dedicated prayer and commitment allows this most meaningful publication to come to fruition. *"The Little Book of Prayers"* offers guidance to the many human casualties littering the roads of life because of their failure to know the direction leading to their destination.

It is scripture and prayer that keeps one aware and in touch with God's presence daily. Prayer becomes the center of a transformed life for the vast majority of Christians who feel powerless in knowing their fate in certainty. The Word of God will give you heavenly wisdom and authority to overcome all satanic attacks, encounters and pitfalls for the divine Word of God has already disarmed the enemy.

I'm indeed proud of your accomplishments, zeal and faith, love of God, commitment to excellence and pastoral ministry in the African Methodist Episcopal Zion Church. The privilege to have nurtured you as a faithful member, Buds of Promise, acolyte, choir member, usher, leader, Young People's Congress President, Varick International Christian Youth Council Executive Vice President, and Young Adults in Christian Ministry Eastern Regional Vice Chairperson and acknowledge you as one of my sons in the ministry is cherished.

Giving this *"The Little Book of Prayers"* the careful and cordial attention it deserves will be of great benefit to all who read it.

May we consistently experience the overcoming power of prevailing prayer and unlock even greater promises as we pray according to the will of God. Remember, "God is able to do exceedingly, abundantly above all that you ask or think, according to the power that worketh in you." (Ephesians 3:20)

The Reverend Dr. Robert L. Graham Sr., Former Pastor
Saint Luke African Methodist Episcopal Zion Church
Buffalo, New York

The prayers by the Rev. Dr. R.J. Chandler, my son in the ministry, carry two powerful suggestions: firstly, the prayers suggest a relationship with God as Father who unconditionally cares for His creation; a relationship with the Father that makes it easy to talk to and with Him. Secondly, the prayers suggest a faith in God that makes believing that God really answers our prayers. These prayers will inspire others to have a closer relationship with God as Father, and a deeper faith in the God who hears and answers our prayers.

The Reverend Dr. Vernon A. Shannon, Pastor
John Wesley African Methodist Episcopal Zion Church
The National Church of Zion Methodism
Washington, D. C.

After reading Reverend Reggie Chandler's *"The Little Book of Prayers"*, the conclusion I've reached is that it is a valuable and insightful tool for clergy and laity. Dr. Chandler does a masterful job in melding the essence of spirituality, scholarship and humility toward a vital prayer life. His meticulous treatise on each aspect of prayer i.e. posture, invocation, petitions and benedictions makes this "Little Book of Prayers" a must spiritual tool for pastors or any other person interested in the spiritual dynamics of prayer.

The Reverend Theodore A. Henderson, Pastor
United States Air Force, Chaplain Lieutenant Colonel (Retired)
Founder of Dover Christian Church
Dover, Delaware

After reading Rev. Dr. R.J. Chandler's *"The Little Book of Prayers"*, I've reached a verdict that dialogue happens when we reach out to God in prayer. Dr. Chandler has laid out the communication channel to which invocation, and petition meet the essence of spirituality. His relationship with God and faith are depicted when we read and feel the power and presence of God through prayer. I believe that these prayers will encourage others to have a daily relationship with the creator.

The Reverend Dr. Baron N. Hopkins Sr, Pastor
United States Army, Chaplain Major
Saint James United Methodist Church
Westover, Maryland

"The Little Book of Prayers" is a unique, down-to-earth, instructional presentation on prayer. Psalms 34:15 states, "The eyes of the Lord are upon the righteous, and his ears are open unto their cry." The psalmist encourages us to pray because the righteous has God's divine approval, tender consideration, and careful attention. Dr. Chandler writes, "Like a brass instrument that communicates beautiful sounds when played properly, prayer can be very effective if we keep our hearts in tune with God." As a musician shines and polishes their instrument, we must work out presenting a communication to God so that He hears beyond our words, but taps into our hearts."

Rev. Dr. R. J. Chandler has written a needed ministry resource on learning the practice of praying different kinds of prayers which include many examples of prayers. If the prayers of the righteous are a sweet melody to God, we can be sure that the Father's quick ear catches each note when our prayers are rightly prayed. May this "Little Book of Prayers" be used throughout the Church.

The Reverend Dr. Otis T. McMillan,
General Secretary Director of the Department of Church
Growth and Development
The African Methodist Episcopal Zion Church
Charlotte, North Carolina

Rev. Dr. Reginald Chandler Sr. does a yeoman job in unearthing some biblical truths that we have glossed over and seem to have forgotten in our hurriedness and dogged pursuit of ritualism. This *"The Little Book of Prayers"* is powerful in its biblical teaching on prayer, practical as a tool for worship, and profitable to the Kingdom of God. Anyone involved in the life of the Church will benefit greatly from this book. I would highly recommend it as a primer for its powerful new and fresh invocations, prayers, and benedictions, but also as fuel for one's own creativity when operating in the area of worship leader or intercessor.

The Reverend Dr. Barbara A LaToison, Pastor

St. Mark African Methodist Episcopal Zion Church

Dallas, TX

Presiding Elder -- Houston-San Antonio and Dallas-Fort Worth Districts

"The Rising Star of Zion"

International President -- Presiding Elder's Council

The African Methodist Episcopal Zion Church

Novices who are learning any kind of practice need to learn the basic rules and guidelines for a practice. This is true whether one is learning how to play the piano, how to play chess, how to swim, or how to practice ministry. Learning the practice of ministry integrates knowing, being, and doing over the course of time. Rev. Dr. R. J. Chandler has written a needed ministry resource on how to learn the practice of praying different kinds of prayers--prayers of invocation, prayers of petition, and prayers of benediction. Along with concise definitions, rules, and guidelines, Dr. Chandler gives a storehouse of prayer examples from his own life of prayer in the practice of ministry. I commend this "little book of prayer" for ministers who have the humility to say as did Jesus' first disciples: "Lord, teach us to pray."

The Reverend Jeffery L. Tribble, Sr., Ph.D.
Associate Professor of Ministry
Columbia Theological Seminary
Decatur, GA
Presiding Elder -- Atlanta District
The African Methodist Episcopal Zion Church

There are no experts in prayer. But sadly, few of us want to be - or admit that we are - beginners. Dr. R.J. Chandler's work helps us all to "begin" the practice of developing the life of prayer such that it will become a habit. And a good habit it is to develop, the habit of sincere, dedicated and committed prayer. Here is an aid to draw us closer to God. Our lives can only be enriched thereby.

The Reverend Dr. Kenneth Q. James, Pastor
Memorial African Methodist Episcopal Zion Church
Rochester, NY

Dean of Conference Studies
Western New York African Methodist Episcopal Zion Annual
Conference
Adjunct Assistant Professor of Preaching
Northeastern Seminary
Rochester, NY

Dr. Reginald Chandler, Sr. has given us a little book with a big impact. This volume gives the Christian and the Church a useful and helpful guide for a weighty, purposeful, and pointed prayer life. Dr. Chandler offers a practical handbook on the importance of prayer in the life of every Christian. His personal lessons are a reflection of a passionate life of ministry which has been on full display for his parishioners, ministry colleagues and all who encounter him. In this book he reveals the fuel for his fire: it is unquestionably the power of prayer. In so doing, he also gives the Church a handbook to use alongside the Bible and the hymnal as tools for deepening the Christian faith through worship and corporate prayer. From the Invocation to the Benediction, Dr. Chandler helps to lift us higher by bringing us deeper. I highly recommend this "little book" to enlarge your prayer life and faith in a big God.

The Reverend Dr. Lester A. McCorn, Pastor
Pennsylvania Avenue African Methodist Episcopal Zion
Church
Baltimore, Maryland

As a scholar, and practitioner of Christian leadership, it is my pleasure to add Dr. Chandler's

"The Little Book of Prayers" to my training repertoire. This tool highlights one of the most essential components to successful Christian ministry: prayer. Current and emerging clergy alike will find this resource beneficial as we continue to develop leaders in the local church and supplementary ministry outposts.

The Reverend Dr. Darius M. Benton, Pastor
Walls Chapel African Methodist Episcopal Zion Church
Houston, Texas

"The Little Book of Prayers" is an instructional, compact tool that will make a major impact on the reader. The author's passion for prayer is laced throughout this manual and will cause the person using it to gain knowledge for their journey ahead. As the Word of God reminds us in Proverbs 27:17, "As iron sharpeneth iron, so a man sharpeneth the countenance of his friend." The Rev. Dr. R.J. Chandler, Sr. is a friend of God and humanity who desires to equip the Body of Christ for such a time as this. Prayer is essential to becoming the effective saints of God we need to be in order to win the battle over satanic forces. I am excited about this new resource and recommend ministers and laypersons alike to add it to their libraries. In addition, it is my prayer that *The Little Book of Prayers* be added to studies within the different levels of the AME Zion Church and even used across

denominational lines. This powerful piece is much too rich to be kept within a small circle of saints, but all should be afforded the opportunity to partake of it and grow together.

The Reverend Dr. Jace L. Cox, Pastor
Founder, Liberty Praise Center
New Bern, North Carolina

Prayer is our most direct expression of communicating with God. Jesus set the example. He taught his disciples the importance and meaning of prayer. *"The Little Book of Prayers"* offer us a plain basic guide to prayer. The author uplifts prayer as a reverent approach to our heavenly Father. In this little, but fortifying text, one can discover the vibrant power of prayer. Look a little closer and learn how to "talk" with the Master in worship services, at meetings, in the early morning hours, in women's groups, in youth and adult groups, at church, in community settings, in prayer meetings. ..everywhere that God dwells. We can take the little book everywhere we go… and find it useful!

The Reverend Geraldine J. Jones, PhD
Author and Free Lance Writer
Director of Christian Education & President W.H.O. M.S
Liberating Power African Methodist Episcopal Zion Church
Bridgeville, DE
Golden Life member of Delta sigma Theta Sorority, Incorporated

One, if not the most important thing in a Christian life is his or her prayer life. Prayer is a vital part of the believer's life because it plays a critical role in how we think of and communicate with God. Dr. Chandler's book, *"The Little Book of Prayers"* is a valuable resource for any believer who is serious about having a healthy, purposeful and rewarding prayer life. It's a life changing book that provides its readers with an instructional and practical way of talking with God from either a private to a corporate setting.

Luke 18:1 says, "Than men always ought to pray and not lose heart." We live in a world today where much prayer is needed, *"The Little Book of Prayer"* is just the thing the people of God need to effectively minister to their families and the world in which they live.

The Reverend Michael L Mills, Pastor
Jordan Memorial Union American Methodist Episcopal Church
Baltimore, Maryland

PROLOGUE

In my twenty years of pastoral experience, two of the most commonly asked questions are:

1) How can I know the will of God for my life? And, 2) how do I hear from God?

Most would agree that effective prayer is an essential part of answering those two burning questions. But, since many struggle in the area of prayer, the practice of prayer becomes a duty to be performed rather than a delight to be enjoyed. *"The Little Book of Prayers"* addresses the process, protocols, and positions of prayer with practical and insightful helps that will encourage its readers HOW to pray effectively and, TO pray consistently. I believe this book will "demystify" the subject of prayer for some, and 'intensify" the experience for others. Undoubtedly, it will justify the time spent to examine its pages.

While this book is a blessing, I am compelled to mention that I just did not read a manuscript sent to me. I have enjoyed the blessed privilege of coming to know Dr. R.J. Chandler Sr. personally. In our times together, it has become apparent that this book flows from a life that is connected to God. Dr. Chandler is a Man of God, a caring Pastor, a devoted family Man, and a joy-filled believer. I am convinced that his book was "lived out" before long before it was "written out." It is with great joy that I commend this book to you. I know that you will gain clarity on what is the will of God for your life, as you hear from Him like never before.

The Reverend Anthony W. Wallace, Senior Pastor
Crossroad Christian Church
Dover, Delaware

CHAPTER ONE

The Introduction

"He was teaching and saying, "Is it not written,
"My house shall be called a House of Prayer for all
nations? But you have made it a den of robbers."
-Mark 11:17

According to *Merriam-Webster's Collegiate Dictionary*, *prayer* is defined as an address or petition to God or a god in word or words used in praying (Merriam-Webster, p.1). It is to make a request in a humble manner. The word *petition* means request. Essentially, to pray is to make a request for something from God. While I agree with this secular definition of prayer, I believe that it is lacking, for prayer is much deeper for the Christian. Prayer is the medium through which humankind communicates with Jehovah, as well as serving as an open dialogue between God and humanity. I believe that anytime one speaks to God, it should be in prayer and supplication (Philippians 4:6).

1

As an instructor of architectural engineering, construction management, and interior design at Delaware Technical Community College, I had the privilege of introducing my students to the Honorable Carlton Carey, mayor of Dover, Delaware, in the 2014 spring semester. I informed them that it was important for them to know what they wanted from him and to be clear and write their questions down on paper. I did not want to waste the time of a high-ranking official with many responsibilities. Additionally, I asked them to dress professionally because they represented themselves and our college. Lastly and most importantly, I asked them to be humble and respectful of the office of the mayor.

If we are to be careful in our approach to people, how much more should we be careful in our approach to Jehovah? The Scriptures suggest that we should come boldly before His throne (Hebrews 4:16) to obtain mercy and grace, but it should always be with reverence. Analogous to the mayor, it is God's prerogative to spend time with us. When the Christian calls upon God, He does not have to answer. Yet, He chooses to answer because He loves us. God does not owe His creation anything, for He has given us everything through the work and love demonstrated on the cross! God is sovereign and unlimited in power. Perhaps that is why the psalmist said, "What is mankind that you are mindful of them, human beings that you care for them?" (Psalm 8:4). The good news is that He does care about our well-being. He cares about our hurts, suffering, dramatic experiences, failures, and pain. However, He also cares about making His promises of joy, love, peace, salvation, and assurance a reality in our lives.

Often I encourage the members of Liberating Power African Methodist Episcopal Zion Church to be clear and get to the point when speaking with God. In God's omniscience, He already knows the desires of our hearts, for David said, "Thou knowest my downsitting and mine uprising, thou understandest my thoughts afar off. Thou compassest my path and my lying down, and art acquainted with all my ways. For there is not a word in my tongue, but, lo, O Lord, thou knowest it altogether" (Psalm 139:2–4 KJV). God knows His creation! He knows our wants, needs, and desires.

He knows our hearts. So you may ask, "If God knows what our needs are before we tell Him, then why do we need to pray? God wants to hear from us. He desires to have an open dialogue with us as it was in the garden of Eden. In the beginning, God and Adam spoke freely to one another, but because of sin, God and Adam were separated.

As we would dress appropriately for the mayor, let us dress spiritually in the attire of meekness, humility, humbleness, gratitude, and non-judgment.

3

> *"Has not my hand made all these things, and so they came*
> *into being?" declares the* LORD. *"These are the ones I*
> *look on with favor: those who are humble and contrite in*
> *spirit, and who tremble at my word." (Isaiah 66:2)*

God favors believers who are humble and contrite in spirit and who tremble at His Word. Let us use the full armor of God as described in the epistle to the Ephesians and make our petitions known to almighty God. Every time we approach the Lord, we should have reverence and awe. When we speak with God, we should speak with respect and dignity. Never mind being star struck by a high-ranking public servant or celebrity. We should be star struck when we meet God at the altar of our hearts.

The Mechanics of Prayer

One Sunday morning during my worship experience, the Lord touched my heart and inspired me to write this little book of prayer to help my fellow clergymen and -women and the laity throughout the church of God. My hope is that this work transcends denominational affiliation and yields itself to the heart of the body of Christ. He allowed me to recognize the importance of prayer, specifically corporate and intercessory prayer. *Corporate prayer* is a term used to describe praying together with large or small groups of people (*allaboutprayer.org*, 2013). Intercessory prayer is when one prays for others. I believe that intercession cannot take place if the intercessor does not embrace redemption. Is humanity redeemable? Is it possible to plead before God on behalf of the sinner and ask Him to release mercy, forgiveness, love, and grace? Can humanity be saved? Are we not all sinners in need of a savior? These questions are not designed to be rhetorical but to cause the Christian to reflect deeply on his or her sinful nature. The truth is that all of His children have sinned and fallen short of His glory (Romans 6:23). Hence, we ought to intercede for one another with purpose, passion, and humility. Intercession is warfare, and we must not handle this responsibility lightly. People's lives are hanging in the balance, and they are in desperate need of God to act. Like for Abraham, God may pause to hear our prayer and dialogue with us as we intercede for family, friends, and loved ones (Genesis 18:23–33).

It's one thing for the Christian to pray on his or her own, but it is something else when one prays in a large gathering of believers. As one begins to utter words unto the Lord in public worship, one takes on the task of approaching the Lord on behalf of the congregation. As Moses, Joshua, and the prophets approached God on behalf of the people, those individuals who utter invocations, pastoral or intercessory prayer (petitions), and benedictions do the same.

This is an awesome and serious task, for the individual who prays for the church is the one who has been selected or singled out to speak to the Lord. It is for this reason that those who have been selected to pray should do an inventory check on their life before they approach the throne of grace.

Prayer

**Lord, create in me a clean heart and
right spirit. Teach me your ways and
lead me toward your truth and grace.**

Chapter Two

Prayer Works When You Work It!

If you believe, you will receive whatever you ask for in prayer.

—Matthew 21:22

Before any person leads a small prayer group or large assembly, I strongly suggest that the leader develops a prayer life. Prayer takes commitment and consistency. Richard Foster, author of the *Celebration of Discipline* stated, "To pray is to change. All who have walked with God have viewed prayer as the main business of their lives. For those explorers in the frontiers of faith, prayer was no little habit tacked on to the periphery of their lives; it was their lives. It was the most serious work of their most productive years. Prayer – nothing draws us closer to the heart of God" (R. Foster, 1988). I would imagine that it is difficult for any worship leader to lead worship in the house of prayer without a prayer life.

How can one be attuned to the spirit if prayer is not celebrated in one's personal daily activities? Before stepping onto the premises of the church, the worship leader should be in prayer.

The Right Reverend W. Darin Moore, bishop in the historic African Methodist Episcopal Zion Church stated, "No routine in 2014!" Too often, Christians make prayer a routine when it should be an extraordinary and unconventional experience. Routine is helpful for one to be disciplined, but it may not enhance one's relationship with God. I'm afraid that many of our worship experiences have become routine and rigid. Perhaps our town meetings with God are too scripted. Our worship should never feel like a rehearsal, but it should be fresh, new, and yielding.

I believe that our individual worship is a reflection of our prayer life. Frequently, I challenge myself by asking the following questions:

1. Is my worship authentic from my heart, or am I just going through the motions?
2. Do I really desire to lay prostrate before the Master's feet and surrender all?
3. Do I worship God in spirit and in truth?

There is much to be learned from daily prayer life, but I highlight three aspects I learned in response to my questions. First, prayer teaches me that I don't have to be in control and that I need to be open to the move of God. Second, prayer teaches me that it does not have to be my way (Isaiah 55:8). Third, prayer teaches me to be patient for God's response. So it is with leading corporate worship. As a worship leader, I should never force my way or allow my agenda to be priority.

Let's go a little deeper. "The Lord says: 'These people come near to me with their mouth and honor me with their lips, but their hearts are far from me. Their worship of me is based on merely human rules they have been taught'" (Isaiah 29:13). Why just simply go through the motions of worship when we have an opportunity to connect with our creator? Why rush the through the worship experience? Is the ritual more important than the relationship?

> *"Each of the four living creatures had six wings and was covered with eyes all around, even under its wings. Day and night they never stop saying: "'Holy, holy, holy is the Lord God Almighty, who was, and is, and is to come." Whenever the living creatures give glory, honor and thanks to him who sits on the throne and who lives for ever and ever, the twenty-four elders fall down before him who sits on the throne and worship him who lives for ever and ever. They lay their crowns before the throne and say: "You are worthy, our Lord and God, to receive glory and honor and power, for you created all things, and by your will they were created and have their being (Revelation 4:8-11)."*

"I've heard laity and clergy say that church does not have to take all day. Maybe it does. Maybe we should diligently seek Him while He may be found and call upon Him while he's yet near. Instead of sticking to a time limit, let us yield to the direction of the Holy Ghost. The Holy Ghost is not bound by time or space. The Holy Ghost is not governed by ritualistic practices or our form of worship. He is not confined to our theological box. Personally, I've experience a powerful outflowing of the Holy Ghost during worship. I wanted to move forward to the next thing, but the Spirit was so heavy and pervasive, that there was nothing I could do but wait until He finished His work on our hearts. The Lord taught me that He's bigger than our feasts, special days and observances. He's bigger than our buildings and ministerial pedestals we allow people to place us on. He's larger than our ego's and limited spiritual view. I believe that prayer is the key in discerning when the worship leader need to step aside and get out of God's way.

The illustration provided by John recorded in Revelation indicates that worship is day and night. It never stops. It is a lifestyle. Though his revelation is of an eschatological phenomena, there is much that we can learn for our present day practice.

1. We learn that just as the four living creatures and elders were created to worship God, we too are created to worship Him.
2. We are made for His pleasure
3. We learn that they were not clock watchers

Should we have long worship experiences? No, unless the Holy Ghost says so. We should have worship experiences that are led by the Holy Ghost, not ritual. Let's prayerfully tune our hearts to the move of the Holy Ghost and make adjustments to the order of worship. The Spirit might lead the worship leader to go from the hymn directly to the sermon. The Spirit might lead the worship leader to replace the sermon with the responsive reading or litany where there is a call and response. The point is that unless the worship leader conducts a daily prayer life and prays during the worship experience, an authentic worship experience may be missed.

It is paramount that the worship leader seeks God about the needs of the church. As stated previously, prayer works when you work it! Not simply praying for oneself, but praying for others. Paul writes to the Church of Ephesus, "Praying at all times in the Spirit, with all prayer and supplication. To that end keep alert with all perseverance, making supplication for all the saints (Ephesians 6:18)." Prayer works especially when we are able to speak to God on someone's behalf. Too often worship leaders place more emphasis on the order of worship than on being in the order of God. Members, visitors and friends come to worship with baggage, infirmities and burdens. They come to the spiritual hospital seeking to be healed and find relief. They are not coming for the preacher or the choir even if they think they are; they are coming to have an encounter with Jesus. People who are tormented by demons and evil spirits, addictions, domestic abuse and traumatic loss scratch and claw their way into the sanctuary. Some are running for their very lives while others are on the verge of giving up. We all need an encounter with the Master. We all need to be filled with the Holy Ghost, but unless the worship leader prays and seeks God, our worship experience will be business as usual. We will miss opportunities for the Holy Ghost to minister because we are more concerned about addressing every item on the bulletin in the order that it is written. A prayer life will create an environment for the worship leader to be in tune with God which the Holy Ghost will take the driver's seat.

Prayer works when we work it. Prayer can change the printed program. Prayer can alter the melodious sounds rendered to God. Prayer can help the preacher preach! Prayer does change things. Prayer can turn a mess into a miracle. Prayer can turn a tragedy into triumph. Prayer can change the flow of a worship experience. Prayer is essential and is necessary for the worship leader to be in harmony with God.

When the Church prays

I am intrigued by The Apostle James's (James5:13-18) views on prayer. In this pericope he teaches on the importance of a praying church. The church which is characterized as a group of believers are encouraged to pray for one another and the unchurched. Conversely, this is the ideal because every person who is inside or outside the body of Christ stands in the need of prayer. Tragedy, misfortune and calamity does not respect one's faith claim. Devastation and destruction will befall the Muslim as well as the Jew; the Roman Catholic as well as the atheist. Seeking God and asking Him to intercede in someone's life in a positive manner is what the Christian ought to do. Regardless of one's views of the supreme deity, I strongly believe that they should be prayed for. Prayer may not remove the problem, but it will grant strength to the believer to get through the season of difficulty. To bring light to this, let us consider the tree. Its three main components are the roots, trunk and branches. Most roots grow deep and spread while the branches reach toward the heaven. When storms come, the tree may sway and bend, but it is not uprooted because it has a strong root. In other words, its foundation is sure. Prayer is the root of the Christian experience. If one has a strong prayer life, then they are rooted and their foundation is sure. Regardless of what life throws at them or the contrary winds of adversity that blows against them, they shall not be moved, for they shall be like a tree planted by the rivers of water (Psalm 1).

The challenges of life will come, just keep on living. I teach my architectural students that when designing a building, one must consider the 100 year flood, 50 year earthquake or 20 year hurricane. These natural "Acts of God" will happen, but we don't know when. The point is to create a building that can withstand the violence of nature. The structure must be sound and anchored to a foundation underground. When unseasonal 100 mph winds begin to howl and threaten to destroy the building, the building will not move nor flinch because of its structural integrity. The same can be applied to a prayer life. You and I have an opportunity right now to develop and design a prayer life that is meaningful. Why wait until the season of persecution or difficulty comes before one starts to pray? Why wait for enemies and demonic forces to overwhelm and corner us before we speak a word of help to our God? Why wait as a church to pray for its saints when we know that its parishioners are struggling to maintain their mortgage, lack of health care or making ends meet during this season of recession? C'mon and let's build something together and pray by pouring the foundational concrete slab while the sun is shining. Let's erect the structure and anchor it to the foundation by praying now while there is still daylight before the night comes. Let's build the roof so that one might be protected from the rain by praying now before the storm comes. For the contrary winds, hail stones, sleet, torrential rains and blizzard will come. I refuse to get caught in the storm without proper attire. One may ask, "How do you do it or what needs to be said?" The answer is simple. Saying thank you is a prayer. Telling God that He is awesome is a prayer. Asking God to help your neighbor is a prayer. Speak of His greatness and salvific power while there is peace in the land so that when war comes, you are already in tune with the Heavenly Commander in Chief.

Prayer does not start at the church, but it begins at home. Our corporate worship should be a reflection of our private devotion. James highlights the importance of a praying church and gives instruction on who should pray for others. He assumes that the congregation will have sick persons among them. He acknowledges that sickness presents a problem that requires a solution. The sickness can be spiritual, mental, emotional or physical. While there are various kinds of sicknesses, the solution is prayer. However, James is careful to suggest that an Elder should lead prayer for others while laying hands on them.

Let's go a little deeper. Before we go any further, let's examine what it means to be sick. Sometimes, there are signs but most often, the signs are elusive. How do we know if we are sick? The story is told of a woman who seemed to be healthy, full of energy and excitement. She was athletic and was a long distance runner. One day, after a morning run she became very ill and coughed up blood. She decided to go to the emergency room at the hospital only to find out that she had stage four cancer. She had no idea that these tumors were growing so rapidly inside her. This sickness did not reveal itself until it was too late. Sometimes sin can hide within us just like cancer. I later learned that the cancer was in her family history. Her aunt, uncle, grandmother and great grandmother all passed at early ages because of this dreadful disease. Like cancer, sin is in our family history because we are the sons and daughters of Adam. Knowing the facts should cause one to get screened regularly. If the cancer can be detected early, then it can be surgically removed or killed by radiation. Christians should make their way to the hospital, which is the Church for their regular screening. We ought to come willingly and lay on the Great Physician's table. The bible says that we are to offer our bodies as a living sacrifice (Romans 12) wholly and acceptable to God. Through prayer, we must endeavor to get on the altar, the table of the Lord and allow Him to proceed with a spiritual surgical procedure. Make no mistake, He's not going to use a scalpel or knife, but He will use a double-edge sword that will separate the soul and spirit and judge the thoughts and intentions of our hearts (Hebrews 4:12). Granny said that He's a doctor in the sick room. He's a lawyer who's never lost a case and a doctor who's never lost a patient.

The Apostle James encouraged the believers to allow the Elders to pray and lay hands on them. The Elders were people of great faith and resolve. These were comprised of deacons, pastors, evangelists, teachers and administrators. The faith of these leaders was tried and tested in the midst of persecution. It is important to note that the early Christian movement participants were persecuted and treated poorly because of their faith in Christ. They believed that following Christ was superior to the law of Judaism, Hellenistic and Roman Cultures. A Christian was looked upon as radical and a threat to the status quo. James understood that the believers, not only were confronted by infirmity, but also violence, mayhem and destruction. The early Christian leaders had to provide a ministry that was relevant, reliable and renewable.

James decided to replicate what He saw in Christ, which made the difference in his effectiveness. Converts were made daily because the Christian leaders mimicked the ministerial method of Christ. My mentor and friend the Rev. Dr. Louis Anthony said that, "The true measure of a disciple is when they can be found teaching what the teacher taught in his or her absence." This displays mastery of the lesson that Jesus taught by word and example. James witnessed Christ praying and laying hands on people. He watched Christ relate and fellowship with others. He studied how Christ provided a word of encouragement and hope from a place of compassion and love. He did not condemn and divide, rather He uplifted and unified. When Christ prayed, He asked God to make the impossible possible and believed it with conviction.

As a pastor, I have to ask myself, "Do I pray with conviction and compassion?" Do I believe that God will answer my prayers for others? Jesus told Peter that the devil asked to sift him as wheat, but that He prayed for him that his faith may not fail (Luke 22:32). This was a prelude to the denial of Christ. Perhaps in another book, we can revisit the question the devil had for Jesus. I believe that Christ recognized Peter's humanity and weakness. Yet, He told Peter that when he turned again, to go strengthen his brothers. My God, this is intercessory prayer at its best! Jesus acknowledged Peter's limitation, but celebrated his promise. I strongly believe that if Jesus did not have this conversation with Peter, then Peter would not have been the vessel used at Pentecost. Peter preached with boldness and power as he was led by the Holy Ghost because he remembered that Jesus told him to strengthen his brothers when he turned. Turn from what? Turn from the lie, guilt, depression, hate, bitterness, loneliness, anger, disillusionment, misery, unfaithfulness, selfishness, pride and fear. This is what the church must do for its members as it is demonstrated by the leadership of the church.

Don't lose the connection

When I attended McKinley High School in Buffalo, NY, I developed many positive friendships with my peers. Out of all of my friends, there was one that I spoke to everyday. We talked on the phone as well as in person through the halls of academia. We had a lot in common so the relationship grew naturally. However, when it was time to graduate, we choose different paths that created a long distance friendship. In time, we lost contact as we both pursued our dreams. Every now and then, we speak to each other through social media but it's not the same. Our closeness is not there. I'm afraid that many Christians treat God the same way. When we are young in Christ as a new convert, our prayer life is consistent and full of great conversation. Unfortunately life happens and we find ourselves not praying as much as we used to.

I am guilty of neglecting my prayer life at times. Yet I pray consistently in large gatherings. This is not healthy because my ear is not in tune with the voice of God. Consequently, my prayers may not be discerning or full of God's power. For this reason, a daily prayer life is paramount.

One of my favorite stories in the bible is that of King Jehoshaphat recorded in the second book of Chronicles.

"Jehoshaphat stood before the community of Judah and Jerusalem in front of the new courtyard at the Temple of the LORD. ⁶He prayed, "O LORD, God of our ancestors, you alone are the God who is in heaven. You are ruler of all the kingdoms of the earth. You are powerful and mighty; no one can stand against you! ⁷ O our God, did you not drive out those who lived in this land when your people Israel arrived? And did you not give this land forever to the descendants of your friend Abraham? ⁸ Your people settled here and built this Temple to honor your name. ⁹ They said, 'Whenever we are faced with any calamity such as war, plague, or famine, we can come to stand in your presence before this Temple where your name is honored. We can cry out to you to save us, and you will hear us and rescue us.'

"And now see what the armies of Ammon, Moab, and Mount Seir are doing. You would not let our ancestors invade those nations when Israel left Egypt, so they went around them and did not destroy them. ¹¹ Now see how they reward us! For they have come to throw us out of your land, which you gave us as an inheritance. ¹² O our God, won't

19

> *you stop them? We are powerless against this mighty army*
> *that is about to attack us. We do not know what to do, but*
> *we are looking to you for help (2 Chron. 2:5-12, NLT)."*

Jehoshaphat was in a difficult predicament and he really needed the Lord. He needed God to move like never before. Jehoshaphat approached God with boldness and expectation. Perhaps he had a consistent prayer life. My high school friendship afforded me certain benefits such as getting help when I needed it, borrowing and having a place to rest my head. Those benefits were awarded because of the relationship that was cultivated each day. If I did not have a relationship, I would feel awkward in asking my friend for anything. I'm confident that my friend would have ill feelings toward me if I always made withdrawals without making any deposits. Our relationship was reciprocal. He knew me and I knew him. Now if I reach out in 2014 and ask him for help, he may ask me "Where have you been since 1995 when we graduated from high school?"

Let us not treat God as a distant friend for He desires to know and commune with us intimately every day. "And the scripture was fulfilled that says, "Abraham believed God, and it was credited to him as righteousness," and he was called God's friend (James2:23 NLT)". The hymn writer Joseph M. Scriven says,

> *"What a friend we have in Jesus, All our sins and griefs to bear!*
> *What a privilege to carry, everything to God in prayer!*

Oh, what peace we often forfeit, Oh, what needless pain we bear,
All because we do not carry, Everything to God in prayer!"

I agree with the hymn writer that the Christian has a friend in Jesus. Not only that, but it is a privilege to carry everything to God in prayer. If God treated humanity as humanity treated Him, where would we be? Who could we run to in the time of storm? How could we live? He accepts us for who we are and listens to our petitions. It is a privilege afforded to us not because we have earned it, but because of His amazing grace. Jehoshaphat was a friend of God and God knew him intimately. Let's take a closer look at Jehoshaphat's prayer. He has an introduction (*Items 1, 2 & 3*), body *(Item 4)* and conclusion *(Item 5)*:

1. *Introduction:* He recognizes that he is speaking to God as the leader of a large group of people. His prayer is inclusive of the people that he is called to serve. It is always proper to use words such as, "Ours, We instead of I and mine" in corporate prayer.

2. *Introduction:* He acknowledges God's sovereignty and awesomeness.

3. *Introduction:* Jehoshaphat reminds God of His promise to the children of Israel. Hence, Jehoshaphat does not make the plea about himself, but it's about the people and their worship in the Temple. When leading prayer, it is helpful for the leader to empty oneself and pray for the needs of others instead of focusing on personal gain or temporal

satisfaction. He admits that the Temple is significant for it is a place where the Israelites can stand in the presence of God.

"And let them make me a sanctuary, that I may dwell in their midst. According to all that I show you concerning the pattern of the tabernacle. And see that you make them after the pattern for them, which is being shown you on the mountain (Exodus 25:8, 9; 40)."

Then he says, "We can cry out to you to save us, and you will hear us and rescue us." He employs scripture and speaks of God's promise in his prayer. Jesus says, "If you abide in me *and my words abide in you,* ask whatever you will, and it shall be done for you (John 15:7)."

4. *Body:* He gets to issue at hand. He gets to the point. He is clear of the needs of the people. Let's not waste God's time but be practical in our theology as we approach the Throne of Grace.

5. *Conclusion:* Lord, help! We don't know what to do, but our eyes are on you. Jehoshaphat is saying, "Lord, I don't know how you are going to do it, but I know it's gonna get done!" Yes, God will make a way out of no way. You and I may not know when, how, where or what, but God will move for our good. God will heal, set free and deliver. He may not come when we want Him, but I guarantee that He will be right on time.

As a leader, we do not need to have all of the answers. We must rely on the word of God. We need His direction and guidance. We must seek His face so that we choose the right path. Our prayers should be engineered in such a way that we do not approach the mercy seat with all the answers. Instead of being empty, we are full. Full of our agenda, full of our plans, full of ourselves. We must diligently evaluate our motives and empty ourselves of our pride, selfishness and self-righteousness.

> *Thus says the LORD: "Heaven is my throne and the earth is my footstool; what is the house which you would build for me, and what is the place of my rest? All these things my hand has made, and so all these things are mine, says the LORD. But this is the man to whom I will look, he that is humble and contrite in spirit, and trembles at my word." (Isaiah 66:1)*

Prayer works when you work it. Let's reconnect with God. In other words, when we take the time to study God's relationship with humanity utilizing the illustrations of the Holy Scripture, we begin to understand that our heart (motive and intent) must be right. Our approach must be that of humility and a contrite spirit. And that we must come as an empty glass ready to be filled with the living water of Christ.

Prayer

"God, open my eyes that I might see my church as You see it. Let me see where change needs to take place, even if it is painful to me. And use me, I pray, to be an instrument of that change whatever the cost (Rainer, T., 2014)."

CHAPTER THREE

The Posture of Prayer

Sometimes when people think of prayer, they think of posture. For example, people would bow their head, bend their knees, close their eyes, and join their hands together. This posture is one of humbleness, humility and reverence. While this is appropriate in corporate and private worship, prayer is not confined to such a position. Also, prayer is not limited to that which is verbal, but it is also intuitive. "With all prayer (Eph. 6:18). All sorts of prayer- public, private, mental, vocal. Do not be diligent in one kind of prayer and negligent in others… let us use all (Wesley, J.)." Prayer should be an ongoing exchange between God and His child not at a designated time, but throughout the day on every day of the week. God is ever present waiting to hear from us.

"I am not a man that looks at the outward appearance, but I look at the heart." – 1 Samuel 16:7

As stated previously, our posture is important, but it is not the determining factor to whether or not God is pleased with our prayer and that it gets answered. Also, the words that we choose to say becomes irrelevant if our heart is not in the right place. I belong to a faith based tradition that believes that God knows our thoughts and ways from afar. One may assume that our thoughts are a reflection of our intent, motive and emotion. Some suggest that this can be identified as the spiritual heart or soul of a man. It is for this reason that humankind must pray unto the Father with a clean heart. If we are honest enough, then we must ask God to create in a clean heart and right spirit (Psalm 51:10).

Paul in his epistle to the church of Phillipi said that we should not worry about anything, but pray about everything. Tell God what we need and thank Him for all that He has done. Consequently, we will experience the peace of God. If we want peace, then we should pray. Grandmomma from the movie *"Soul Food"* said, "Ain't no need of praying if you are going to worry... Ain't no need of worrying if you are going to pray (Tillman, 1997)!"

Several years ago when I was living in Buffalo, New York, I would spend time with my nephew Devonte taking him to church activities. On a Sunday afternoon after the benediction was given and the parishioners were dismissed, he decided to run around on the second level of the church. All I could hear was the pitter-patter of little feet running back and forth down the hall. My mother finally caught him at the foot of the stair and asked him a question with a stern voice, "What do you think you were doing?" Devonte's response was, "I was looking for God." While I am pretty sure that he was not looking for God, he did have a valid excuse as to why he was running around. I am very thankful that the presence of God is not confined or limited. God is everywhere. He is omni-present. In other words, we do not have to run looking for God in different rooms of the church or think that we have to speak to God in places that humanity have identified as sanctuaries. The prophet Jeremiah asked the question, "Can a man hide himself in secret places so that I cannot see him? Declares the Lord. Do I not fill heaven and earth? Declares the Lord (Jeremiah 23:24)." Proverbs 15:3 reminds us that "the eyes of the Lord are in every place, keeping watch on the evil and the good."

It is unfortunate that some Christians do not pray outside the four walls of the church building. Some do not pray at all because they believe that prayer should be for sinners. Conversely, others take on the attitude that God is too Holy and pure to stoop to their level of sin to listen to them; let alone take them serious. I believe that these mindsets are incorrect and far from the truth. The bible declares in the epistle to the Romans (6:23) that all have fallen short of the glory to God. No human being except Jesus is exempt from sin for we sin by thought, word and deed. This is not a onetime occurrence but it happens daily. The truth of the matter is that God knows that His children will make mistakes and miss the mark of His holy standard. It is for this reason that Christ died for all humanity so that we could be reconciled unto God. God made the impossible, possible. It was impossible for God to hear our prayers because of sin without a blood sacrifice. The blood sacrifice was the Lamb of God.

Thanks be to God for His Son Jesus, the Lamb who became the ultimate blood sacrifice. "For God was reconciling the world to Himself in Christ, not counting people's sins against them. And He has committed to us the message of reconciliation (2 Corinthians 5:19)." God made it possible for all of His children to come to Him just as we are whether that means broken, hurt, mischievous, hateful, murderous, prideful, arrogant, lustful, etc. No matter what sins we have committed, if we approach the Father with reverence, respect and a repentant heart, the bible says that He will hear us and respond no matter where we are. The writer of 2 Chronicles reminded the Israelites that if my people, who are called by my name, will humble themselves and pray and seek my face and turn from their wicked ways, then I will hear from heaven, and I will forgive their sin and heal their land (7:14). Let us seek to humble ourselves for He will lift us up (James 4:10).

We must challenge ourselves to make sure that our heart is in the right place no matter what our sinful condition is. That means acknowledging God as Creator and Master of the universe. Furthermore, we must acknowledge that He is the epitome of love and that it endures forever. Remember that God does not have to recognize our prayers or respond to them, but <u>He does</u> and <u>He will</u> according to our faith because He loves us and desires to be in intimate loving relationship with us.

Praying in tongues

Book of Discipline of the African
Methodist Episcopal Zion Church

Article XV - Of Speaking in the Congregation in Such a Tongue as the People Understand

It is a thing plainly repugnant to the Word of God, and the custom of the primitive church, to have public prayer in the church, or to minister the Sacraments, in a tongue not understood by the people.

"The one who speaks in a tongue builds up himself, but the one who prophesies builds up the church. Now I want you all to speak in tongues, but even more to prophesy. The one who prophesies is greater than the one who speaks in tongues, unless someone interprets, so that the church may be built up. Now, brothers, if I come to you speaking

in tongues, how will I benefit you unless I bring you some revelation or knowledge or prophecy or teaching? If even lifeless instruments, such as the flute or the harp, do not give distinct notes, how will anyone know what is played? And if the bugle gives an indistinct sound, who will get ready for battle? So with yourselves, if with your tongue you utter speech that is not intelligible, how will anyone know what is said? For you will be speaking into the air. There are doubtless many different languages in the world, and none is without meaning, but if I do not know the meaning of the language, I will be a foreigner to the speaker and the speaker a foreigner to me. So with yourselves, since you are eager for manifestations of the Spirit, strive to excel in building up the church.

1 Corinthians 4:4-12

The Apostle Paul seems to compare the speaking of tongues and prophesy in his epistle to the Church of Corinth. He asserts that the edification of the church is paramount. Prophesy improves the Body of Christ. However, the speaking of tongues can also build the body of Christ when there is someone to interpret. Paul seems to suggest that it is appropriate to speak in tongues when praying to God privately. One is permitted to build faith not in a selfish act, but in an intimate exchange with God. Speaking tongues should be performed in a manner where God is glorified in an isolated setting unless it is interpreted for the edification of the church.

When praying publically, we should caution ourselves not to speak in a language that the body of Christ cannot understand. Our corporate prayers are not for self-gratification. Hence our language should be clear, concise but creative; creative in the sense that the individual praying should be relevant and use examples that the people within the prayer circle can relate to. The very essence of speaking in tongues is uttering words in a different language that is unknown to the person praying. It is important to note that speaking in tongues is a gift of the Holy Spirit. Some will have the gift of speaking in tongues and others will not.

> *But to each one is given the manifestation of the Spirit for the common good. For to one is given the word of wisdom through the Spirit, and to another the word of knowledge according to the same Spirit; to another faith by the same Spirit, and to another gifts of healing by the one Spirit, and to another the effecting of miracles, and to another prophecy, and to another the distinguishing of spirits, to another various kinds of tongues, and to another the interpretation of tongues. But one and the same Spirit works all these things, distributing to each one individually just as He wills.*
>
> *1 Corinthians 12:7-11*

The principle purpose of speaking in tongues is to communicate with God. It is important throughout our churches that we do our very best to align with scripture and not with the wiles of popular doctrinal propaganda that has become the gospel of what sounds good. Let us be careful not to compromise our fundamental beliefs in the pursuit of trickery and entertainment in the pulpit. We are not called to be actors and actresses that put on a show of our intellectual prowess or ability to speak quickly as if our tongue is like a machine gun that rapidly unloads a magazine. We are called to be dispensers of the Gospel of Reconciliation. In a public setting, let us endeavor to speak a language that the listener can understand. Let us seek to build up the Body of Christ utilizing words that are familiar to their ear for the bible says that faith comes by hearing and hearing the word of God (Romans 10:17 KJ).

Chapter Four

Invocations

Bless the LORD, O my soul: and all that
is within me, bless his holy name.
- Psalm 103:1

Invocations are typically short one to two minute prayers uttered at the commencement of the worship experience requesting God to commune with His saints as we offer up our sacrifice of worship, praise and thanksgiving.

To invoke is to invite. I believe that it is dangerous if one should assume that just because they are offering God worship and praise, that He accepts it. How can one begin to worship God without first acknowledging who He is and asking Him to be in their midst? Please understand that if God should decide to spend time with us as we worship Him, then we should count ourselves privileged. God does not have to stop by our Sunday morning worship or any other gathering and He will not come if He is not invited.

Invoking the presence of God Almighty

Here we are O Lord unified by one spirit and one baptism requesting that you come and commune with us here in this place. Lord, you are welcome. We invoke thy Holy Spirit to move from heart to heart and breast to breast. Fill us O Lord with thy liberating power as we attempt to offer our praise, love and worship to your name. Touch us on this great occasion that we set aside this time to be revived, renewed, and reenergized and we will be so careful to give you the glory. In Jesus' name… Amen.

Children's Day

Thank you Lord for this beautiful day. We pause to invoke thy Holy Spirit to share with us as we give our best worship and praise of your Holy name. We ask that you rest, rule and have your way in this place as we honor our children on the special occasion called, "Children's Day." Help us to recognize how precious they are in your sight and that we must lead and guide them according to your teachings and principles of love. In Jesus' name… Amen.

Men's Day: Congregational (in unison)

Gracious Father, we thank thee for your love, grace and mercy. We invoke thy Holy Spirit to be with us in our Men's Day worship as we attempt to worship in spirit and truth. Transform, empower and mold us into the men and women you are calling for in times of distress so that we may be a beacon of light to a world of darkness. In Jesus' Name, we pray. Amen

Youth Sunday

Oh Lord, thank you for your benevolence and love that you have bestowed upon us. We also thank you for allowing us to worship you in freedom and hope. We invoke thy presence to be with us during our Youth Sunday Worship Service as we celebrate your faithfulness through song, dance and praise. In Jesus' name. Amen.

Missions Sunday

We are tremendously favored to call upon your name boldly because of Jesus Christ. Please come Holy Spirit and have your way. In faith, we thank you for being with us. We ask for a special touch of your grace as we direct our focus to Missions this day. Renew our minds and refuel our spirits to carry out the work of reconciliation. In Jesus' name, we pray. Amen.

O Father God, we have assembled ourselves together to commune and fellowship with you. We invoke the Holy Ghost to be with us as we worship and celebrate who you are. Help us to embrace our salvation and liberation by the power of the words of Jesus. Please help us to understand that in order for us to be revived in the spirit; we must acknowledge that our spirit needs reviving. In Jesus' name... Amen.

Thank you dear Lord for your love, direction and favor upon our lives. Through your mighty acts and faithfulness, you have displayed how wonderful and forgiving you are. Your grace and mercy is sufficient for us. We invoke your presence dear Lord. As we have attempted to bless you, you have undeniably blessed us through song, scripture, prayer and preaching on days past. Therefore, through faith, we expect you to do another great work in us at this hour. In Jesus' name... Amen.

> *Yet a time is coming and now has come when the true worshippers will worship the Father in spirit and truth, for they are the kind of worshippers the Father seeks. God is spirit and His worshippers must worship in spirit and in truth.*
>
> *John 4:23-24*

O thou great Jehovah, we thank you heavenly Father for thy goodness and mercy. We thank you for thy dear Son Jesus Christ that through Him, you have allowed humanity to be reconciled unto you. As we worship you, we ask that you would be with us in our midst and receive sacrifice of thanksgiving and praise. In Jesus' name…. Amen.

Father, we invoke and ask that you come into this place. We thank you for your mighty acts of love and faithfulness. Help us to celebrate your goodness, grace and mercy. Accept our praise oh Lord as we open our hearts to receive what you have in store for us. In Jesus' name…. Amen.

O gracious loving Father… We thy humble servants thank you for being who you are in our lives. You are King, Almighty, and Everlasting. We invoke the presence of the Holy Ghost to be in our midst during our order of worship and service to you. Our prayer is that you will be pleased with sacrifices of our bodies, praise and financial gifts. Have your way in this place. Teach us, move us, convict us, motivate us, empower us, help us and bless us in Jesus' name. Amen.

Good morning Lord. We thank you for allowing us to see another beautiful day. We invite the presence of the Holy Spirit to be with us as we attempt to worship and praise you with our hearts, minds and spirits. Please move freely to inspire, encourage and love your children. Especially your young people. In Jesus' name. Amen.

Gracious Father, we thank thee that because of the decision you made to create humanity in your image; we are your children. Lord you are invited to be with us at this hour. Please accept our invitation. Try our hearts and remove the blockage of sin. Teach us your ways and decrees. Train our hands for your purpose. In Jesus' name. Amen.

Dear Heavenly Father, that you for this day. As the result of your grace and mercy, you have allowed us to rise out of our beds clothed in our right mind. Thank you for allowing us to see one another's face as we have come to worship you in spirit and truth. We invoke the Holy Spirit to be in our midst in our congregational worship experience as we dare to be different in our lifestyle of sanctification, salvation and wholeness. In Jesus' name. Amen.

Lord, you are welcome in this place. Fill us with thy quickening power and love as we celebrate who you are to us. Please have your way in this, thy holy tabernacle as we offer up our sacrifice of praise and thanksgiving. In Jesus' name. Amen.

CHAPTER FIVE

Petition

Pray unto the Lord

"One day Jesus was praying in a certain place. When
He finished, one of His disciples said to Him, "Lord,
teach us to pray, just as John taught his disciples."
Luke 11:1

We should never allow ourselves to get to a point in our
spiritual growth that we stop asking the Lord to teach us to
pray. Regardless of our age or office in the church, there will
always be something that we can learn about prayer. Prayer never
gets old. Like a brass instrument that communicates beautiful
sounds when played properly, prayer can be very effective if we
keep our hearts in tune with God. As a musician shines and
polishes his or her instrument, we must work out presenting a
communication to God so that He hears beyond our words, but

taps into our hearts. Remember that our words are inadequate. The English language as well as others is limited. The question becomes, "What's going on with our hearts?" God spoke through the prophet Isaiah "These people come near to me with their mouth and honor me with their lips, but their hearts are far from me (Isaiah 29:13).

Make no mistake; the condition of my heart is more important than the words that are coming from my lips. This applies to personal as well as corporate worship. Typically, petitions are made for groups of people. When leading the prayer for large gatherings, the prayer warrior or intercessor ought to check their intentions and motives. It is not the concern of the prayer leader to know the state of each person's heart within the circle. Their concern should be the purity of their heart. In most scenarios throughout the bible, God speaks to a leader and in turn, the leader speaks to a large group of individuals.

As one prays publicly, it is helpful to use words such as, "Us or we rather than I or me." The intercessor should use words in the plural form to benefit the group or congregation.

It is imperative to our spiritual growth that we are honest with the Lord for in most cases; we do not know what to pray for or how to ask. Our words are inadequate to explain our love and devotion to Him. Truly our words come short in explaining His majestic wondrous ways.

Jesus answered His disciples by introducing what we refer to as the Lord's Prayer. I believe that it is a great model prayer for all of God's children whether juvenile or seasoned.

"The Lord's Prayer!"
Our Father, who art in heaven, hallowed be they name,
Thy kingdom come, thy will be done on earth,
As it is in heaven. Give us this day,
Our daily bread, and forgive us of our trespasses,
As we forgive those who trespass against us,
And lead us not into temptation, but deliver us from
Evil. For thine is the kingdom, and the power, and the
Glory forever, Amen.

1. **Acknowledge and thank God** – His sovereignty, power, parental guidance. He is the author and finisher of our faith. In Him we move and have our being. He is the beginning of all things for everything was made for His pleasure. We must thank Him for who He is and what He has done for us. "Thanksgiving is inseparable from true prayer; it is almost essentially connected with it. One who always prays is ever giving praise, whether in ease or pain, both for prosperity and for the greatest adversity. He blesses God for all things, looks on them as coming from Him, and receives them for His sake- not choosing nor refusing, liking or disliking, anything, but only as it is agreeable or disagreeable to His perfect will (Wesley, J.)."

Every prayer should begin with thanksgiving. "In everything give thanks: for this is the will of God in Christ Jesus (1 Thess. 5:18 KJV)." Christians have much to be thankful for such as: the breath of life, temporal material goods, health, family, employment, salvation, love, etc. Surely, there is something that we can be thankful about. For all that the Lord has done for and through us. We ought to be thankful. If the Lord decides to withhold His blessings for us, we should still be thankful for all that He has given us in the gift of eternal life. We should be thankful for being saved and delivered from our sins.

2. **Follow God's will** – Ask God to help us do His will on earth as it is done in heaven. Obedience, loyalty, honor, integrity and commitment are attributes that will help Christians to be true to God. Jesus prayed in the Garden of Gethsemane and asked His Father to "Let this cup pass from Him..." Then Jesus said, "Not my will, but thy will be done!" It's not about us, but it is about Him. When the Christian confessed with their mouth and believed in their heart (Romans 10:9, 10) that God raised Jesus from the dead, they committed to the law of Christ. That is, He has bought us with a price so we are to glorify Him (1 Corinthians 6:20) with our bodies. I belong to Christ. My mind, body and soul belongs to Him. Hence, I am obligated to follow His will. As a result of the wickedness and sinful nature, I need help in following His will. Thanks be to God who spoke to us through the Prophet Ezekiel,

"For I will gather you up from all nations and bring you home again to your land. Then I will sprinkle you clean water on you, and you will be clean. Your filth will be washed away, and you will no longer worship idols. And I will give you a new heart, and I will put a new spirit in you. I will take out your stony, stubborn heart and give you a tender, responsive heart. And I will put my Spirit in you so that you will follow my decrees and be careful to obey my regulations (Ezekiel 36:25-27)."

Let's be honest with God and stop acting as if we have it all together. Let's remove the masks that hide our true identity. Let's be real with God and allow Him to take us just as we are. Through the avenue of prayer, our communion with Him will be life changing, refreshing and renewing if we approach the mercy seat as a wretch undone.

3. **Acknowledge God's Providence** – Recognize that He is Jehovah Jireh "The Lord our Provider." As He fed the Israelites manna from heaven, He shall feed His children the living bread which is Christ Jesus.

We don't have all of the answers, but we like to think we do. We need God's help. We need His provisions. We need His answers. We need His guidance for He will lead us as our Shepherd to better pastures. The Apostle Paul told the Church of Phillipi that God will supply our every needs according to His riches and glory through Christ Jesus (Phil. 4:19).

4.   **<u>Acknowledge God's mercy and grace</u>** – How can we ask for forgiveness when we do not forgive? How can we hope that God is merciful when we do not demonstrate mercy to others? Truly it is difficult to forgive others. However, with the help of the Holy Ghost we can forgive and show mercy to anyone who trespass against us. How can we pray with a clear an open mind when we hold a grudge, resentment, bitterness or hate against our brother or sister? All of God's children need of mercy. Our enemies need prayer too.

> "A Christian community either lives by the intercessory prayers of its members for one another, or the community will be destroyed. I can no longer condemn or hate other Christians for whom I pray, no matter how much trouble they cause me. In intercessory prayer the face that may have been strange and intolerable to me is transformed into the face of one for whom Christ died, the face of a pardoned sinner. That is a blessed discover for the Christian who is beginning to offer intercessory prayer for others. As far as we are concerned, there is no dislike, no

personal tension, no disunity or strife that cannot be overcome by intercessory prayer. Intercessory prayer is the purifying bath into which the individual and community must enter every day."

- Dietrich Bonhoeffer

5. <u>**Acknowledge that temptation is real**</u> – Though temptation comes in all forms for it is anything that persuades us to go against God's holy standard. Temptation will lead us to evil. The hymn writer said that we are prone to wander. For this reason, we must diligently ask God to deliver us not from the temptation, but from the evil that is the consequence of the temptation. Being made in the image of God, we are in His likeness. The ability to choose, reason and to create are attributes of His likeness. Hence, God gives humanity free will to choose His will over our will. Our will is sown in flesh, but His will is of the spirit. Our will shall lead us into darkness, but His will shall lead us to the light. My will can cause me to choose to overly consume alcoholic beverages

6. <u>**Acknowledge God's Salvific Power**</u> – It's all about His kingdom... His power... His glory! Not just for now, but forever. We are saved through grace because of the work that was accomplished at the cross. We are redeemed and set free by the blood of the Lamb of God, Jesus Christ. Through Him we are declared justified, righteous and a new creature.

Petition of Consolation in Pregnancy

Let us pray. You are awesome and your ways are amazing. Thank you Lord for your many blessings such as the gift of life, the love of our families and the hope through Jesus Christ our Lord. We pray dear Lord that the delivery of this baby will be successful and healthy. Your daughter is tired and she desires rest from this pregnancy. We believe through faith that she will give birth to purpose. Grant her strength to push. Remind her that her miracle is on the way if she does not give up. Bless her and her husband as they prepare for the delivery of this gift. Remind them that the child is your gift to them, but they must present their child as a gift to you by raising the baby according to the biblical principles and admonition of the Lord. In Jesus' name. Amen.

Prayer for call of action

O dear merciful Father, we they humble servants beseech thee to commune with us here in this place. We desire thy fatherly goodness and presence as we attempt to worship you in spirit and truth. Today is the day that you have made... Therefore, we rejoice and we are grateful. We ask O God that you would empower us as we accept the great commission of Christ to go ye therefore to every nation... every community... every neighborhood... every city block and baptize in the name of the Father, Son and Holy Ghost. In Jesus' name... Amen.

Prayer for call of action

O Heavenly Father, thank you for your goodness, grace and mercy. You are AWESOME in all your ways. Your loving kindness endures forever. Great is your name in all the earth! Jehovah… We need you. The Psalm writer declared, "In God, whose word I praise, in God I trust; I will not be afraid. What can mortal man do to me (Psalm 56:4)?" Lord, we trust you. We praise your word and shall not be afraid. Please loose peace and assurance; may it fall on the hearts of every parent or guardian whose child is missing throughout the world. We need your hand of deliverance.

Prayer for call of action

Please perform a miraculous wonder in the safe return of our children. Please send thy Holy Spirit and move throughout the world in our homes, communities and regional areas and do a sweeping. From the jungles of the Congo to the metropolis of capitalism, we implore you to intercede in the affairs of humanity and provide hope to the hopeless, victory to the victim, health to the sick, and love to the broken hearted. Child abduction, juvenile abuse and human trafficking are some of the atrocities of evil throughout the world that must be confronted utilizing the blood of Jesus.

Prayer for call of action

Oh God, I believe that you are calling the Church of God to action! Loose our tongues so that we are not silent! Open our hands so that we may use them to build your kingdom. Open our hearts so that we may be compassionate, empathetic, loving and sensitive as Jesus. Increase our faith to believe that with God, "All things are possible!" Give us that Jericho praise that through our praise and marching, the walls of injustice and tyranny will crumble. Give us that Davidic faith that though we don't have much, we will still use what we got to destroy the enemy. With God on our side, we are not the minority, we are the majority. Help us to be mindful of what Jesus said, "I am sending you out like sheep among wolves. Therefore be as shrewd as snakes and as innocent as doves (Matthew 10:16)." Give us direction. Send thy Holy Ghost to lead and guide us as we preach, teach and share the Gospel of Reconciliation. Now is the time for action! Use us for thy service dear Lord. Thank you for hearing our prayer. In Jesus' name. Amen.

Prayer of Hope

Heavenly Father, we thank you for life and the ability to see. We thank you for family and for comfort. This journey called life gets difficult sometimes but, through faith we believe that you are with us. In your time dear Lord, we ask that you reveal to us your will for our lives and the direction that you would have us to go. In Jesus' name. Amen.

Prayer of Hope

Dear God, the Psalmist said, "I call on you, my God, for you will answer me; turn your ear to me and hear my prayer (Psalm 17:6)." Hear our prayer, O Lord, hear our prayer, O Lord, incline your ear to us, and grant us your peace. Amen.

Petition of God's Providence

Heavenly Father, you are the source of our strength. In you we live, move and have our being. You are awesome and glorious in all your ways. We thank you for life, love and hope through your Son Jesus. We pray that you would strengthen the families across the world in ways that only you can. Father you know what we stand in need of. Please provide it. Lord you know our stories and what we've been through; our good times and bad times. Our rising and sitting. You know our thoughts from afar and you are acquainted with every hair on our heads. You know us for you made us and you care. You care about our anxiety, sickness and depression. You care about the little things that make us smile and the obstacles and challenges of life that makes us afraid or doubtful. What is humanity that you are mindful of us? Thank you for providing a way when there is no way. Thank you for opening doors, clearing pathways and giving us direction. Thank you for being our cloud by day and our pillar of fire at night. Thank you for supplying all of our needs according to your riches in glory. Thank you for speaking to our hearts and providing a way out of temptation. Thank you for your faithfulness, grace and mercy. In Jesus' Name. Amen.

Prayer of Thanksgiving

Lord, I have been thinking about you lately…. How are you? I hope that you are doing well. I know that you are busy in the midst of your children around the world. That's why I just wanted to thank you Lord for being intimate with me no matter what's going on. You always have time for me. I thank you for your love and tender mercies that I attempt to embrace every day. I thank you for your unconditional love and support that you give me in spite of my foolish ways. Surely, you are wonderful and gracious. I cannot begin to count my blessings for there are too many. My frail finite ways cannot comprehend your ways. Thank you Lord. Amen.

Petition of Forgiveness

O thou great Jehovah, please forgive and be merciful unto us. We apologize for our reckless and inconsistent behavior.

We have missed thy perfect standard in our work, play and conduct. Help us Holy Ghost to live a life that is pleasing to you by how we live and be treating our fellow brother or sister with the love of Jesus. Please forgive us of our sins, create in us a clean heart and a right spirit. Jehovah Rohi (Psalm 23:1), you are our good shepherd that will lead us to the path of righteousness. You will lead us to the land flowing with milk and honey. You will lead us to the place where we are satisfied. Your scriptures are true; there is no perfect gift that you would keep from us. However, our despicable and terrible ways grieve the Holy Ghost. Please forgive us... We continue hurt people and speak ill-will toward our enemies. Please forgive us. We don't help the poor and visit orphans as we should. Please forgive us. We forget about our brothers and sisters who are incarcerated. How hard is it for us to send a note in the mail to encourage them? Please forgive us. Forgive us of our bad attitude, calloused heart and scandalous. Forgive us for not praying enough for strangers who are in need. Forgive us for being an instigator that speaks violence instead of peace. Jesus is the Prince of Peace (Isaiah). Jesus taught us to be peace makers, yet we have created chaos in our families, on our jobs and in the communities. Please forgive us because most times, we do not know what we do until the damage is done. We need you Jehovah Rophe (Exodus 15:26) to heal our land, tame our tongues (James) and clean our hearts with the blood of Jesus. We are grateful that we can come boldly before the mercy seat and ask for forgiveness.

This is the confidence we have in approaching God; that if we ask anything according to His will, He hears us. And if we know that He hears us — whatever we ask — we know that we have what we asked of Him.

- 1 John 5:14-15

Prayer of Forgiveness

Please forgive me Jesus. It's me, its me standing in the need of prayer. My Savior, My God and King. Emmanuel, I need you this hour. I have sinned and fallen short of your perfect standard. I am a wretch undone. I've sinned by thought, word and deed. Please do not leave me Lord. I recognize that you are Holy and pure. I am nothing but filthy rags. Like Paul (Romans 7) the good that I desire to do, I don't do. What I don't want to do, I do. My flesh is weak. Forgive me for allowing my mind to wander and not subjecting it to the power of the Holy Ghost. Forgive me for being fickle in my faith and foolish in my ways. Forgive me Lord for stumbling into the same pit that you rescued me from. I know I shouldn't be there... I know I shouldn't go near it... But that sin keeps calling my name... "Lord have mercy!" Help me to face my enemy and stand firm like Jehoshaphat (2 Chron. 20) for I've been fighting my battles long enough. It's time for me to allow you to fight my battle. You are Jehovah Nissi (Exodus 17:15), my warrior King who will help me in my time of trouble. Please strengthen my faith...

Build my character. Please give me new vision and wisdom so that I may act in ways that are according to your will. Lord, I desire to give you the best of my time, talent and treasures. I surrender all to you. Please accept my offering and hear my prayer. In Jesus' name. Amen.

Prayer of Forgiveness

Thank you Lord for your forgiveness. I don't deserve it... I can't earn it... I can't pay for it... Teach me how to repent and mean it for You are faithful though I am fickle. Help me Jesus to get it right for the bible says, "You are forgiving and good, O Lord, abounding in love to all who call on you." — Psalm 86:5. Lord, teach me to live by the Spirit every day. Help me to please you in every way. My thoughts... my actions... my words.... Send thy presence oh Lord for I am mindful of the scripture, "Live by the Spirit, and you will not gratify the desires of the sinful nature." — Galatians 5:16. In Jesus' name. Amen.

Petition of Healing

Father we pray in the name of Jesus for my dear sister and friend in her time of need. May she and her mother be comforted with the hope that is in the healing power of Jesus. You are the great physician... The doctor who has never lost a patient. Please move by your Spirit in the emergency room. Guide each health care practitioner, anoint them with wisdom. Sweep the room of any bacteria that will cause harm. Bless them with that calm assurance that all is well and that this too shall pass. I thank you for your faithfulness and mercy. In Jesus' name. Amen

Petition of Healing

Heavenly Father, thank you for your goodness, awesome healing power and miraculous ways. We ask in the name of Jesus that you touch him or her. Restore, comfort and heal their body. Refresh their mind and grant them peace and assurance. You are faithful and true. We believe that all shall be well. Please reignite our faith in you to know that the doctors, nurses, healthcare practitioners, and technicians work for you. Because the Holy Ghost is in charge, all things will work to the good for us who are called by your purpose. Thank you for what you are doing right now. In Jesus' name, Amen.

Petition of Healing

Father, in the name of Jesus, I ask that you bless this child. Please heal their body and remove the infirmity. Please touch and comfort her as we know that this sickness is difficult for her.

Please bless the parent as he or she is used by you as the facilitator of healing. In Jesus' name. Amen

Petition of Hope

Lord, you are amazing! You are good. Hallelujah. You are the King of Kings and the Lord of Lords. Our hope is built on nothing less, than Jesus blood and righteousness. There is none like you. No one can touch my heart like you do. In you there is hope. You are the hope of our salvation. As a result of the death and resurrection of thy dear Son Jesus Christ, all of your children who have declared Jesus as their Lord have a right to the throne of grace and mercy. We are grateful that we can boldly come before you. Thank you dear Lord. We do not need a priest to intercede on our behalf for Jesus is our high priest. He is our advocate who shall stand with us and declare that we are not guilty though we have committed many sins. He is our mediator and we thank you for being a lawyer who has never lost a case. Thank you for hope for it is what we hold on to. We hope that tomorrow will be better than today. We hope that there is a bright side somewhere. Hope that when that ol' ship of Zion that has landed a many of thousand will come to pick us up. Hope that when the Master returns (Revelation 21), Jesus will wipe away every tear; pain will desist from troubling us; fear will be gone and forgiveness will abound. Hope that we will take residence in that room that Jesus talked about in John 14.

Petition for Humanity

O sovereign God. You are merciful and mighty. Your ways are wonderful. We thank you for our family and friends. We ask that you bless every person in a mighty way. In times like these, we pray that all peoples of every color, creed, gender and lifestyle would come to know you for themselves. You are so good to your children. You abound in forgiveness and unconditional love. Your will is perfect and for us. We pray that people will come to know you so that they can walk in the fullness and integrity of the Spirit. It is our hope that all of humanity would walk toward the resurrection of Jesus and try you. We believe that people are running from something that they do not understand. We don't understand why you died for us… We don't understand why you love us so much… We don't understand why there is so much evil in the world… We don't understand why you forgive us over and over. However, what some of us do understand is that you have given your children the bible which is a record of your relationship with humanity throughout the ages of time. We can see how forgiving, just, loving and fathering you are to all creation. Thank you. In Jesus' name. Amen.

> *And when you pray, do not be like the hypocrites, for they love to pray standing in the synagogues and on the street corners seen by men. I tell you the truth, they have received their reward in full. But when you pray, go into your room, close the door and pray to your Father, who*

is unseen. Then your Father, who sees what is done in secret, will reward you. And when you pray, do not keep on babbling like pagans, for they think they will be heard because of many words. Do not be like them, for your Father knows what you need before you ask Him.

Matthew 6:5-8

Get to the point!

Let us endeavor to get to the point. What is the bottom line? The words we use in prayer should be meaningful and direct. It is not necessary for us to, 'be around the bush,' but get to the heart of the matter. The quality of our words is far more important than the quantity. Jesus said that "A good man brings good things out of the good stored up in his heart, and an evil man brings evil things out of the evil stored up in his heart. For the mouth speaks what the heart is full of (Luke 6:45)." God knows our motives and inner desires. Using fancy words, spiritual tongues and loud speaking may impress the flesh, but it does not impress the Lord. What does impress Him is how we pray according to our faith and believing in what we ask for. We must do our best to approach the mercy seat humbly and with humility.

Before I pray publicly or lead an intercessory prayer for a congregation, I found it helpful to ask myself the following questions:

1. Who am I praying for?
2. What am I praying for?
3. Why am I praying for these individuals?
4. How shall I approach the Lord on their behalf?
5. What do I expect to happen?

These steps have helped me to focus my intent. God is King and sovereign and should be treated with respect, honor and dignity. I attempt to be very careful as to how I approach the throne of grace not just for others, but also for myself.

Chapter Six

Benedictions

Farewell my beloved

*May the grace of the Lord Jesus Christ,
and the love of God, and the fellowship
of the Holy Spirit be with you all.*

2 Corinthians 13:14

The Oxford University Dictionary defines benediction as, "the utterance or bestowing of a blessing, especially at the end of a religious service (Oxford, p. 1)." It' origin is late Middle English from *benedicere* which means to wish well or bless. I often remind parishioners that they should never leave without the final blessing. As the corporate worship service to God concludes, the minister has a major responsibility to pray God's blessings upon the people before they leave. We must remember that while people feel a sense of freedom of expression, love and warmth in the service, it is unlikely that they will receive the same outside the doors of the church. It is for this reason that the final prayer should act as the spiritual covering that will keep them until the next meeting.

> *Again Jesus said, "Peace be with you! As the Father has sent me, I am sending you." And with that He breathed on them and said, "Receive the Holy Spirit."*
> *John 20:21-22*

As Jesus sent out His disciples, the Pastor, Evangelist, Elder, Bishop or Apostle of the assembly sends out the congregation into the community to serve and be an agent of love. Though there is safety and love within the fellowship, there is danger, evil and hate outside of it.

In the Hebrew Scriptures, we find Melcheizedek the high priest pronounce the benediction over the life of Abram. Melcheizedek's authority is underscored as he is the acting agent of God used to speak a word of hope over the life of Abram. The promise belonged to Abram for he was chosen by God to be the patriarch of the faith, but in the office of high priest, Abram came to know the blessing of the benediction (Hebrews 7:1, 6, 7). Hence, God has selected the preacher and endowed them with authority to pronounce blessings to the flock of God. The benediction conveys God's promises, peace and power. Additionally, it communicates His faithfulness and love that is everlasting.

Benedictions

"The Lord shall preserve thee from all evil. He shall preserve thy soul. The Lord shall preserve thy going out and thy coming in from this time forth, and even for evermore (Psalm 121:7, 8)." Amen.

"Now the God of hope fill you with all joy and peace in believing, that ye may abound in hope, through the power of the Holy Ghost (Romans 15:13)."

"Now unto Him who is able to keep you from falling and to present you faultless before His throne with exceedingly great joy; to the only true wise God, our Lord to Him have majesty, dominion and power henceforth now and forever more. Amen (Jude 1:24, 25)."

Now we are the gathered people of God, but soon we shall be the scattered people of God. Remember that tomorrow is not promised so make every effort to smile, speak a kind word and give a hug of love to a brother or sister. May God bless you, hold you and keep you. In the name of our Lord and Savior Jesus Christ, let all God's people say, Amen.

"God shall supply all you need according to His riches in glory by Christ Jesus. Now unto God and our Father be glory forever and ever. Amen (Philippians 4:19, 20)."

My beloved, we have come this far by faith, but we have much further to go. Be aware and on guard for the evil one will attempt to sift us as wheat, but do not fret for the Lord Jesus has prayed for us. May His grace, mercy and love keep you till we meet again. In Jesus' name. Amen.

"Grace and peace be multiplied unto you through the knowledge of God, and of Jesus our Lord. According as His divine power hath given unto us all things that pertain to life and godliness, through the knowledge of Him that hath called us to glory and virtue (2 Peter 1:2, 3)."

"Now the God of peace, that brought again from the dead our Lord Jesus, that great shepherd of the sheep, through the blood of the everlasting covenant, make you perfect in every good work to do His will, working in you that which is well pleasing in His sight, through Jesus Christ; to whom be glory forever and ever. Amen (Hebrews 13:20, 21)."

"The grace of the Lord Jesus Christ, and the love of God, and the communion of the Holy Ghost, be with you all. Amen (2 Corinthians 13:14)."

Aaronic Blessing: "The Lord bless thee, and keep thee. The Lord make His face to shine upon thee, and be gracious unto thee. The Lord lift up His countenance upon thee, and give thee peace. Amen (Numbers 6:24-26)."

"Finally brethren, be perfect, be of good comfort, be of one mind, live in peace; and the God of love and peace shall be with you. Amen (2 Corinthians 13:11)."

God be merciful to thee and bless thee and cause His face to shine upon thee. Amen.

"Now may our God and Father Himself, and our Lord Jesus Christ, direct our way to you. And may the Lord make you increase and abound in love to one another and to all, just as we do to you, so that He may establish your hearts blameless in holiness before our God and Father at the coming of our Lord Jesus Christ with all the saints (1 Thessalonians 3:11-13)."

"Now may the Lord of peace Himself give you peace always in every way. The Lord be with you all (2 Thessalonians 3:16)."

CHAPTER SEVEN

God's Response

Then you will call on Me and go and pray
to Me, and I will listen to you."
Jeremiah 29:12

Does God respond to our prayers? Is He really listening to our cries, petitions and questions? How will God respond? When will God speak to me? Why is He taking so long to answer? When He speaks, how will I know it's Him and not my imagination? Will He speak with a loud thunder or will His voice be like a calm whisper?

With so many unanswered questions, I'm afraid that many Christians slowly lose interest in praying consistently. Who likes to wait for God to respond especially when He may take years; decades or even centuries before He says two words? The hard truth is that time does not belong to us, rather it belongs to God

(Psalm 90:4). We are on His time. He created time and space in His sovereignty. He transcends time. He is the master architect who is not bound by 24 hours, day or night. He is the day and the night. He is who He is.

He is "The great I AM (Exodus 3:14; John 8:58)." His word is a calculated and strategic power with purpose at His pleasure. Human rhetoric cannot describe Him, people can't define Him and the devil can't stop Him. He is God! Supreme ruler, loving Savior, Omnipotent Healer, a Battle Axe, Defender and Deliverer. In His creative genius, whatever He speaks comes to pass for His word will never return to Him void. In spite of Christians losing their interest in prayer, God never loses His interest in us. He never loses His concern for hearing and answering our prayers.

Does God respond to our prayers? Yes. When He is good and ready, He will respond. Job prayed to God and it seemed like his prayers were not making it to heaven. He was sending up timber, but nothing was coming back down to him. He cursed his birth after losing his possessions, children, dignity and wealth. God watched silently. Job struggled through adversity, pain and loss. He received poor counsel from people who loved him. Yet God was silent. From chapter two until chapter 38, God was silent. Whenever God is ready to speak, He speaks with authority. God provides an answer that I'm sure that Job was not expecting.

"Who is this that darkeneth counsel By words without knowledge? Gird up now thy loins like a man; For I will demand of thee, and declare thou unto me. Where wast thou when I laid the foundations of the earth? Declare, if thou hast understanding."

Job 38:2-4 ASV

It's alright to question God. Just be sure that you open your heart to receive His answer. He is not limited in what medium He employs to communicate His message. He can use the Scriptures from the bible, fiction and nonfiction books, climatic conditions, people, animals, nature, dreams, signs and visions just to name several. God responded to Job's prayer out of a whirlwind. He responded to Moses utilizing a burning bush (Exodus 3:4). He responded to Hannah's prayer through the priest Eli when he told her, "Go in peace, and the God of Israel grant your petition which you have asked of Him (1 Samuel 1:17)." God answers prayer. God responded to Hezekiah's prayer through the preacher and granted him 15 more years after he refused to die (Isaiah 38:5). When the Israelites were taken into Babylonian captivity and they cried out to God, God told them to chill out and relax in their bondage. He instructed them to build houses and dwell in them; plant gardens and eat their fruit. God reminded them that He knows the thoughts that He thinks towards them, thoughts of peace and not of evil, to grant a future and a hope... (Jeremiah 29:11). God will answer the prayers of His children.

The Prophet and worship leader Habakkuk asked God, "O Jehovah, how long shall I cry, and thou wilt not hear? I cry out unto thee of violence, and thou wilt not save (Habakkuk 1:2)." God waited. He did not respond as quickly as the prophet wanted him to, but God took His time. When God was ready to respond, He told Habakkuk to write the vision and make it plain upon the tablets because the vision was for an appointed time. Though the vision may tarry, wait for it because it is coming (Habakkuk 2:2, 3).

The Meantime

Why does God seem to take a long time to answer prayer? I believe that God wants His children to practice faith. Every Christian will experience a "meantime." In the meantime, we should endeavor to wait patiently. In the meantime, we practice faith and we work. To illustrate this point, the story is told of a father and son. The son sent a text message to his father asking him to take him to the movies to see Ninja Turtles. The father never responded. The little boy sent him another text and tagged it with a red flag. Still, the father did not respond to the text. The little boy grew impatient, frustrated and annoyed that his father did not respond to him quickly. As he was sitting in his unkept room, he began to tap his foot and mumble. The father soon returned home and walked into his son's room. He told his son that he was ready to take him to see the movie until he saw the messy room and smelled the odor. The father said, "We can't go to the movie with your room like this!" To the sons amazement, he said, "Well daddy, I wish you would have texted me back and told me to clean my room." The father responded, "I shouldn't have to tell you about cleaning your room because you already know my expectations. While you were waiting, you could have been working. Your request is not denied, but it is delayed. Do your part because I always do mine." In many cases, God's response is not of denial, but the Christian may have to wait because we are not ready to receive what He has for us. We may not be able to handle the blessing with spiritual maturity and responsibility. Simply, it may not be our time or season.

I thank God for the meantime. The meantime:

1. Helps the Christian to grow closer to God.
2. Encourages the Christian to have total dependency on God
3. Challenges the Christian to practice patience through prayer

The meantime helps the Christian to grow closer to God. Paul admonishes the Church of Ephesus (Ephesians 6:18) to never stop praying to God. Frequently in the Old Testament scrimmages between Israel and the enemies of God, Israel won because of prayer. Contrarily, when prayer was not priority they lost. Paul was incarcerated when he wrote his letter to the Ephesians. Scholars suggests that he did not pray for his release or temporal satisfaction, but he prayed that God might reveal the mystery of the Gospel. Consequently as one grows closer to God, one's perspective changes about their circumstance. The question alters from, "Why am I here to what do you want me to learn from this!" The meantime fosters an environment for spiritual growth, renewal and restoration. As the Christian matures, they embrace the wisdom of King Solomon when he wrote, "Trust in the Lord and lean not unto thy own understanding. In all your ways acknowledge Him and He shall direct your paths (Proverbs 3:3-5)."

Growth also comes from experiencing the God moment. A God moment is when the Christian is able to see the workmanship of the Lord in their life. I call this life unexplainable blessings that happen to us beyond our control. The good news is that Christians will experience many God moments in their lives. This too happens in the meantime.

The meantime encourages the Christian to have total dependency on God. Jesus said to His disciples not to worry about what to eat, drink, wear or live (Matthew 6:25-34) because the Lord has it under control. He told them to look at God's agricultural and habitat handiwork. He asserted that if God takes care of that which is less significant than human beings that are made in His image (Genesis 1:26), surely God will take care of His most prized creation. The hymn writer said that God will take care of you. I believe that the meantime helps the Christian refocus our vision so that we can see clearly where our help comes from.

The meantime challenges the Christian to practice patience through prayer. Patience is an essential characteristic of Christ that we must learn.

Can you hear God's voice?

> *And he said, Go forth, and stand upon the mount before Jehovah. And, behold, Jehovah passed by, and a great and strong wind rent the mountains, and brake in pieces the rocks before Jehovah; but Jehovah was not in the wind: and after the wind an earthquake; but Jehovah was not in the earthquake: and after the earthquake a fire; but Jehovah was not in the fire: and after the fire a still small voice. And it was so, when Elijah heard it, that he wrapped his face in his mantle, and went out, and stood in the entrance of the cave. And, behold, there came a voice unto him, and said, What doest thou here, Elijah?*
> *1 Kings 19:11-13*

God's voice is mysterious. I believe that consistent heartfelt prayer brings us closer to discerning the voice of God. Sometimes His voice will be thunderous and other times, it will be small and still. As stated previously, God is not limited in the methodology of communicating His truth. We must diligently pray and ask God to open our hearts and minds to His Word. As the scriptures teach us to test the spirit of humanity by the Spirit of God, let us test what we think is the response of God by the Word of God. Does God's response align with the scriptures in the bible? Is there consistency? I've learned that God operates within His own parameters. His parameters is love. The Christian has a moral obligation to ask themselves if the response of God is rooted in love. Can one identify the fruit of the Spirit (Galatians 5:22) which is in fact the characteristics of Christ?

If one continues to have difficulty in hearing God's voice, I recommend following the example of Samuel in the Hebrew Scriptures. Samuel heard the voice of the Lord calling his name and thought that it was the priest Eli. After numerous attempts made by Samuel to inquire what Eli needed, Eli discerned that it was God calling the little boy. Christian mentors are very helpful in interpreting the voice of God.

The Praying Church

There is an African Proverb, "The family that prays together stays together!" The same can be true for the church. The church that prays together stays together. Renowned Christian author

Thom Rainer suggested in his book, *"The Autopsy of a Deceased Church"* that one of the many reasons that churches die is because they fail to pray with each other consistently. Prayer is extremely important as it is the life blood of the church. The church is a living organism and unless it prays, it will die. In the Acts of the Holy Spirit, we find Peter in prison (Acts 12) waiting to stand trial. A remnant of church members came together on one accord and prayed for the release of Peter. The bible says that Peter received the visitation of an angel late in the evening. God dispatched His angelic host from on high and sent him to Peter on assignment. The good news of the Gospel is that every believer has an angel that is assigned to him or her. Notice that Luke does not suggest that Peter prayed for his release but that the church folk prayed. There is power when the church prays. Something happens when the church forgets or lay aside their own needs in order to agree on one need. I wonder what would happen if the church rejected self-interest and yielded to the common good. I wonder what would happen if the church became like-minded and unified under one faith and one baptism before they approached the mercy seat of God.

I believe that the church would return back to the place of holy boldness where she is not afraid to call sin, sin. If the church prayed consistently, I believe that she would take her rightful place as a leader of social action and justice in the local, state and global community. I am grateful for social service organizations but make no mistake, Jesus commissioned the church to look after the widows and orphans, the disenfranchised and the homeless, the less fortunate, down trodden and weary laden. Prayer can change things. If the church prayed like it ought to pray, then there would be no fear or timidity amongst all Protestant denominations and the Roman Catholic Church in addressing the current trends and lifestyles that are contrary to scripture.

Demonology and evil spirits are real and we must not back down, but confront it with the word of God as the standard. I pray that the universal church would come together in keeping our urban and rural streets safe as well as our elementary and high schools safe from evil minded people who should not have a firearm. Terrorism, domestic abuse and pedophilia are demonic forces that are plaguing multiracial communities and it seems as if the church is silent. Divorce and the destruction of the family; the first ordained institution of God has become common practice. I am reminded of when the disciples attempted to exorcise a demon and they failed. They asked Jesus why they couldn't remove the enemy. Jesus told them that some things cannot happen except by prayer and fasting. As I stated earlier in this manuscript, prayer works when we work it! President Barack Obama stated that we are the change that we are looking for. Let's go back to basics and return to prayer. God will hear and respond for the prayers of the righteous availith much. Let us remove the idols of hypocrisy, entertainment and gimmicks in the pulpit and make the church what Christ called, "The House of Prayer!"

As in the days of the church of Acts, the universal church of today is under attack. Church attendance is low. The needs of the congregants are not being met. There is a very low percentage of young adults actively participating in worship. Older or more seasoned members are dying off. The millennial generation have different needs than the baby boomers such as social media, sermon downloads, video conferencing through Skype, Facetime and Fuze.com, shorter worship services, contemporary music, different dress code and motivated through inspiration instead of humiliation. Prayer can change things.

We serve a relevant God though our forms of worship may be irrelevant. God still speaks and He responds to our prayers but are we listening? He is speaking through the changing of the times, but are we listening? He is speaking through the unseasonal weather but are we listening? Are we too busy to listen? Do we actively seek quiet moments for meditation and reflection where we are alone and intimate with God? Often Jesus would steal away (Luke 5:16) to be alone with God. He excused Himself from the busyness of ministry and temporal responsibilities. He left His sheep in order to spend time with the Shepherd of shepherds. No matter how many people Jesus touched, blessed, preached or performed a miracle for, he always intentionally took time to pray alone. I believe that every Christian needs some alone time. Perhaps Jesus could not raise the dead if He did not have some alone time. Maybe He would not have walked on water if He did not have some alone time. Conceivably, he would not have preached with power had He not had some alone time with God. I believe that the Christian needs the alone time with God as much as the human being needs oxygen to live.

Final Prayer

O God you are sovereign and there is none like you. Thank you for life, health and strength. Thank you for the Spirit that intercedes for me. Thank you for Jesus who has prayed for me. Teach me how to love you, love others and please you with my time, talent, and treasures. Teach me how to serve humanity like Christ. Help me to be a catalyst for change and prevent me from being a stumbling block to the Holy Spirit. Lead me oh great Jehovah and order my footsteps. Bridle my tongue that I may speak words of love and healing. Deliver us from evil and the traps of the devil. In Jesus' name. Amen.

ACKNOWLEDGEMENTS

I thank God for allowing me the privilege of writing about prayer. Though there have been countless articles and books on the subject, prayer never becomes exhausted, outdated or out of touch because it is always relevant. There is always more to learn if we open our hearts to the instruction of the Holy Ghost.

I thank my wife Shameka for her love, continued support and for praying for me. She is the wind beneath my wings. Your grace and class captivates me and I thank God that I belong to you and you belong to me. Thank you for blessing me with four beautiful children: Reginald Jermayne Jr., Riley Josiah, Reid Jeremiah and Raelyn Joy, I love you so much. To my grandfather Leroy Fraiser (deceased) who taught me to never give up and work hard, I am grateful. To my grandmother Helen Fraiser (deceased) who I remember fondly telling me not to be a jack-legged preacher, I thank her for believing in me. To my parents Don and Delores Chandler who unequivocally encourage and support me with advice, critique, direction and love, I thank you. Daddy, I pray that I will be as good of a father to my children as you are to me. Thank you for being my life-coach and hero. Mom, I pray that I will make you proud and be the man that you raised me to be. To my father and mother-in-law Bill and Sharon Fletcher, I thank you for your acts of kindness, love and support. To my extended family and friends, I thank you.

To my pastoral charge Liberating Power African Methodist Episcopal Zion Church, I thank you. It is an honor to pastor great citizens of the Kingdom of God in this vineyard of Zion.

I am deeply appreciative of every preacher who provided words of encouragement to me for this work. It means a lot to me that you sacrificed time to read this manuscript. Thank you Bishop Richard K. Thompson for your kind words rendered for the *Foreword*. Thank you Bishop Michael A. Frencher and Bishop Samuel C. Ekemam for your words of love and inspiration. To my friend and mentor Rev. Anthony Wallace, I thank you for your words of benevolence in the *Prologue*. My father's in the ministry never cease to amaze me in the personhood of the Rev. Dr. Robert L. Graham Sr. and the Rev. Dr. Vernon A. Shannon. The two of you never stifled, but pushed me to be the best that I could be. As a young preacher, you accepted me for my uniqueness while directing me toward greatness. I thank you Dr. Graham for teaching me administration, strategic planning and team building. I thank you Dr. Shannon for teaching me how to smell like the sheep. I shall never forget your words, "That anybody can preach, but everybody can't pastor!"

My hope is that this work will be a blessing to the Church of God. I pray that the reader will draw closer to God through the empowering of the Holy Ghost. Let us all seek to find ways as to how we can enhance our prayer life through the example of Jesus by the utilization of the disciplines of meditation, fasting, solitude, study and reflection.

REFERENCES

Andy. (2013). Dietrich Bonhoeffer on the Power of intercessory Prayer. Retrieved from www.biblegateway.com

Benediction. (2014). Oxford University Dictionary. Retrieved from www.oxforddictionaries.com

Corporate Prayer. (2015). Retrieved from http://www.allaboutprayer.org/corporate-prayer.htm

Foster, R. (1988). *Celebration of discipline: The path to spiritual growth* (Rev. 1st ed.). San Francisco: Harper & Row.

James 2:23. (2014). New Living Translation: Bible Gateway. Retrieved from https://www.biblegateway.com/passage/?search=James%202:23

Jeremiah, D. (2013). *The Jeremiah Study Bible*. Worthy Publishing.

Prayer. (2014.) Merriam Webster Collegiate Dictionary. Retrieved from Merriam-webster.com

Rainer, T. (2014). *Autopsy of a Deceased Church: 12 Ways to Keep Yours Alive*. Nashville: B&H Publishing Group.

Scriven., J. (1855). "What a friend we have in Jesus." Retrieved from <u>http://library.timelesstruths.org/music/ What a Friend We Have in Jesus/</u>

Tillman, G. (1997). *Soul Food*. Fox 2000 Pictures

Wesley, J. (2007). How to pray: The Best of John Wesley on Prayer. Barbour Publishing. Uhrichsville, Oh.

The African Methodist Episcopal Zion Church. (2012). *the Book of Discipline of the African Methodist Episcopal Zion Church* (1st rev. ed.). Charlotte, NC. A.M.E. Zion Publishing House

Printed in the United States
By Bookmasters